A Journey into the Soulful Garden

Canada Geese fly in formation and are always
helping one another to stay on course.

So should it be with humankind.

A Journey into the Soulful Garden

Connecting Spirit with Nature

L.M. Taylor

iUniverse, Inc.
New York   Bloomington

A Journey into the Soulful Garden
Connecting Spirit with Nature

iUniverse books may be ordered through booksellers or by contacting:

iUniverse
1663 Liberty Drive
Bloomington, IN 47403
www.iuniverse.com
1-800-Authors (1-800-288-4677)

Because of the dynamic nature of the Internet, any Web addresses or links contained in this book may have changed since publication and may no longer be valid.

ISBN: 978-1-4502-0292-3 (sc)
ISBN: 978-1-4502-0290-9 (dj)
ISBN: 978-1-4502-0291-6 (ebk)

Library of Congress Control Number: 2009913887

Printed in the United States of America

iUniverse rev. date: 3/29/2010

ALSO BY L. M. Taylor

A Guide to Becoming a Vegetarian
Cranbrook, British Columbia
Canada
Copyright 1986

Gardens West Magazine
Featured Article, March 1998, Vol. 12 No 2
Vancouver, British Columbia
Canada

ALOHA FROM ALL THOSE
ON THIS JOURNEY

Love & Aloha
is in all of us
Open your heart
and you'll find it

MAHALO
THANK YOU

DEDICATION

This book is dedicated to the memory of my father, George, and mother, Helen. Also to my loving and supportive children, Andrew and Claire, and to my extended family.

Special thanks to Mary Ann, Joan, Kim, Leslie, and Chantal for helping prepare the manuscript for submission with many source materials, and for their ongoing encouragement.

Thanks to Andy for the many adventures on the Island of Molokai.

I give my deepest respect to Paramahansa Yogananda for opening up my heart and mind to love, beauty, and wisdom.

I would like to honor NaLeo, beautiful singing angels, who have talent beyond imagination: their music preserves the traditions of Hawaii and brings joy to the entire world. This includes their newest CD, *Where I Live, There Are Rainbows*. Their appreciation of nature and song has been a great inspiration to me in my stories.

I would like to extend my appreciation to and credit these talented photographers. Thank you for your permission. E.J. Peiker for "Standing Bear" and "Climbing Tree Bear," http://www.ejphoto.com. The real "Indigo the Bear" by the apple tree was taken by the author. Rod Taylor for "Henry the Deer" with the author, and Bill Ayrton for "Henry the Deer with Chimes."

Waves of thanks to Veronique, the photographer for the "Mule Deer," "Plumeria Flower," "Face of the Gosling," and "Swimming Dolphins." She also contributed to the design and layout.

For creating happiness, love, and joy in my life, my little flower of an angel cat.
Thank you, Salem!

He Mau Huelo Hau' oli ia^ ' Oe!
Happy Tails to You!

PRAISE PAGE

The garden brings life, beauty, and a connection to the earth. These stories are refreshingly candid and pleasantly entertaining.
—Louise LeBlanc

The messages are lessons in hearing the hum of the universe. Often, people talk to the animals. Very seldom do we listen. Thanks for being the one who listens. These stories made my heart sing. I smiled the whole way through!
—Kim Parsons

I can't believe the relationship with the deer and the gander. Wow!
—Carole K. Boyd

Whether it's the sparrows who nest safely under the deck, the tenacious squirrels who race the birds for seeds and nuts along the railing while playing slalom between the feeders, or the vibrant jays who screech high up in the trees, waiting for the familiar sounds of peanuts crashing to rest on the deck's new stone surface, the animals surely must feel welcome at Creekside Gardens.

They're certainly not without company around the deck, let alone in the garden. But it's the deer who rule the gardens, at least when there aren't any bears around! They line up along the fence to munch on many an apple, move around to snack on the bushes along the side of the shrubs, and a brave few will even climb right down to the hedge just outside the patio doors for a special treat. One friend stands out. It's Henry, a young buck Lynda's been feeding since he was but a fawn. I've heard tales of intimate encounters between the two, with Lynda feeding him out of hand at the back porch. The enduring one, however, was when Henry got tangled up in some wind chimes in the fall. He let Lynda remove a chime with little protest as it was dangerously near his eye.

Lynda consistently shows her spirit, speaking to the animals like old friends, with love and honesty. It's like something out of a movie: the yard teaming with wildlife and an array of changing shades from the turf and trees that cycle with the seasons.
—John Helm, B. Com. Writer

Imagine this: you wake up on a bright, sunny morning, grab your book and tea, and head out to the gardens. You settle in on a comfortable garden chair amidst brilliant hues of gorgeous flowers. The setting is perfect, the fragrances wafting in the gentle breeze. Pure bliss! Something catches your attention, and you look up again to discover that you are not alone in the garden this morning. Three beautiful deer are lying a mere fifteen feet away from your chair. One of the deer stares directly into your eyes, and silent communication begins.

The kindness and compassion radiating from the deer into my body was heartwarming and touching. I felt open, alive, and at one with nature—completely blessed and filled with a sense of profound peace. This was a moment to remember and cherish forever in Lynda's gardens. Opening our hearts to the beauty around us, we will experience tremendous healing and happiness.
—Elizabeth Manuel, B Ed. CACE, Happiness Coach and Author

CONNECTING SPIRIT WITH NATURE

The greatness of a nation and its moral progress
can be judged by the way its animals are treated.
—Gandhi

This book is dedicated to all animal lovers and gardeners around the world who have shared their knowledge, appreciation, and sensitivity from their souls to the souls of those who do not speak our language but can communicate nonetheless. Listening and being in the presence of nature is an uplifting gift. It's a treasure chest of wisdom that will help us connect to our real selves. Nature's bounty is endless and provides entertainment that can soothe the soul.

The most amazing things can happen when we believe in the importance of showing gratitude to our beloved and unpredictable Mother Nature. When we realize this great truth, that we are but a living whole, a droplet of divinity, we can be great stewards to our nature friends anywhere and at anytime.

An impressive thought:
At the end of life, I want to leave with my eyes closed and my heart open.

The most important question to ask yourself:
How much have I loved this life?

Use random acts of kindness daily:
Spread your kindness with a smile, a blessing, a flower, or a thought.

For humans and creatures of this planet:
Help someone or something in need to make things better. Rescue a spider and release it outside or send a healing or happy thought to someone who is upset. All these things will start a rejuvenating cycle that will keep going like a spiral around the world.

To interact rightfully in the natural world:
Be respectful and don't willfully harm anyone or anything.

There is one Link, one Life eternal, which unites everything in the universe—animate and inanimate. One way of Life, flowing through everything.
                    —Paramahansa Yogananda

Contents

Chapter One
a lesson in magic
Henry the Mule Deer

DEER TRACKS

A special day about woods and deer tracks

Rain-softened mud
showed clear deer tracks
where mother and little one
earlier crossed my path.

One set smaller
wandering back and forth
among the steadier, larger tracks.

I stopped, stooped and
placed the vee of my spread fingers
in one of the tracks
and felt the deer.

The next rain will flatten
all the mud again, and erase
these sharp prints.

I realized that my foot prints
will also disappear
but it was all right,

Better; at once
I was free, unfettered.
I walked along
counting the minutes of
my great day.

By Henry Burt Stevens
www.authorsden.com

It was early March. I felt extremely cool. Crispness was in the air when I stepped out from the atrium onto the porch landing. A blackish shadow caught my attention out of the corner of my eye. Focusing my gaze, I noticed there were several bucks and a few female deer grazing on the grass approximately twenty feet away. A few quickly scurried around the corner by the brilliant blue giant spruce trees near the creek, fearful of my presence. As I stood perfectly still, one young deer seemed to have no apprehension at all and walked in a beeline in my direction. I turned away from the deer and walked back inside. I had an old metal bucket on the floor. I filled it with a critter crunch wildlife food mix and cut up a few apples. I was now ready to feed the deer.

The deer waited patiently at the porch for my return. Had he tried this before with another human or was this just a coincidence? I moved along quietly to meet him outside the atrium door to the back stone steps.

With an outstretched hand, I offered a delectable treat of seeds. He finished three handfuls quickly. I relished the experience of this close encounter with this magnificent creature. I decided to get a larger bucket to see what would happen. This time, I had a little more seed to offer him. He went on to polish off several more handfuls until he was satisfied. Deer have double stomachs like cows and do not have to digest their food immediately. I assumed my hand would be a wet, slimy mess and smell unpleasant. To my surprise, there was no odor of any kind. My hand was perfectly clean. A long, soft tongue gently stroked my hand a few more times; all the while, I studied his body for any distinguishing marks that made him different from the others. This buck needed a name. What seemed appropriate to me at this moment was Henry.

The remaining herd, with large, globelike, piercing, black Bambi eyes, stayed close. They stared at me, trying to figure out how he got food and they did not. They were skittish and rightly so. This is the way nature prefers it. Then Henry walked away, and so did the rest. I sent a silent communication: "I enjoyed your visit; come again."

On another occasion, I was taking a water container out to the garden shed for storage some seventy feet away. After placing the container on the ground in the shed, I gathered up a blue-handled watering can. Henry appeared suddenly, antlers and all, from behind the Mountain Ash tree at the shed's entrance. I had not heard him at all, so this moving shadow startled me. It took my breath away for a moment. I recognized his markings. He had a fuller face than the others, the largest ears that I had ever seen, and two half-broken-off antlers from either jostling with other males or scraping off bark from a tree.

The path leading to the atrium was snow-covered. He joined me in stride and walked a well-worn path of fresh hoof prints to the bag of grains sitting on the porch. Only one yard separated us. This was a really smart buck, no doubt about that. He had me pegged as a real softy. I did not mind at all, for a special bond had been established to something in the wild, and it was magically displayed by Mr. Henry.

I learned some time later that deer have a familiar route that they visit daily. I see him at least twice a week. I may miss the odd few days. A favorite time for their visits is at dusk, under cover.

I had just filled my peanut butter feeder earlier that morning. Several holes were drilled into a short wooden log to hold the food, and the log is hung up for mother nature's feathered friends. Later that afternoon, a deer was on the porch and was happily licking away all of the peanut butter from the feeder. Upon witnessing this, I thought it best to move the feeder to a higher perch. I have heard from others and noticed from my own experience that deer enjoy unsalted peanut butter on apples, corn on the cob, bananas, and even watermelon.

I wanted to see if Henry would let me touch his chin, cheek, or forehead. He did willingly, and the light gray hairs that covered his face and body were soft to the touch. Some clumps of hair had fallen to the ground because of molting in the spring. I picked it up to look at it more closely, noticing a crimping pattern. This hair resembled miniature baffles, like insulated curtains that cover windows, perhaps for warmth!

The next fall, I was tidying up my herb garden with a statuesque Saint Francis presiding over the bed. I was focused on covering the last lavender plants for the winter, when I heard some chimes. I did not have any chimes in my back garden area. I carefully peered up from the fragrant lavenders to hear this sound again. In the next moment what stepped forward was a sight to see. I could not believe my eyes. Chimes were wrapped around the antlers of a buck. One-foot-long dangling metal tubes and a square piece of wood were pasted across its forehead. I had to laugh to myself. How often would you ever see something like this? I wondered if anyone would notice their chimes were missing.

It was moving toward me slowly but was afraid. One of the foot-long chime tubes was hitting him directly in his right eye. He was squinting, shaking, and tossing his head around. I felt he was desperate. *Is this a sign I am supposed to do something?* I hurried back to the house for some bird seed and very sharp, small, red hand pruners. I decided against using knives, scissors, or loppers. At this time of season, the antlers are just tender blood vessels with a soft velvet covering and are extremely sensitive.

Bending down on one knee, I could see the black threads from the chimes were wrapped tightly around the antlers many times. It was squeezing the antlers so tight, they were bulging a bit. This had to hurt. I held out my left hand, which was full of seeds, and he started to eat. With my right hand that held my clippers, I took a very quick snip. It was a lucky clean cut, and the one tube fell down on the grass, leaving his eye free. If the chime had hit a stepping stone, it would have sounded a noise and the buck could have bolted. I thought of this later. I felt the need to take care of this situation. He seemed happy, I am guessing because he was relieved of some pain.

Henry had enough of me pulling on his sensitive antlers. He turned gracefully around and walked down the path, out of sight. Still hanging from the antlers was a small piece of wood and three foot-long tubes attached by nylon strings, chiming away. It made me laugh, but I was sympathetic to his situation. *Would the other bucks think he was special?* Maybe females would be more attracted to him. Perhaps he would be recognized as the leader of the group because he had something exclusively unique that the others did not have. A local newspaper displayed a picture of Henry with a comment from Bill, an avid photographer and his friend, Cam, who together captured this great moment.

After speaking to the conservation officer in our area, I was informed that it had been quite a year. Another buck was reported carrying around a tomato cage attached to its antlers and another one with a children's inflatable inner tube around its neck. I heard that another trusted human being was able to feed the buck and snatch the tomato cage off. I truly do not feel anyone could attempt the inner tube removal!

When a buck's antlers lose their soft, furry, velvet covering, the new bone growth continues to harden in a very short time, like petrified wood, making them not so sensitive. When bucks rub their antlers up against trees, they not only mark their territory by scraping the bark off trees but they can completely remove their antlers.

Henry returned the following week, still with the musical chimes dangling around his antlers, now more twisted than ever. He came close, and I made another attempt to remove them but failed. He trusted me one more time, but I was again unsuccessful. This was all the attention he could handle and walked away. After this meeting, several weeks passed before I saw him again.

Auspiciously, he returned, and I thought it was a different buck because I was expecting to see one with the chimes clinging to its head. After closer inspection, I noticed that red tuft on the head and a wide, gray face as he walked in my direction. There were no chimes anywhere, but no other buck had ever walked directly to me. It was then I knew for sure it was my Henry. The company he came with kept their distance.

The shriveled, burgundy-colored crab apples from winter's freeze were lying on the ground and softening. Indeed, they were the favorite appetizers of four-legged animals. A blush apple wine is ready on the uppermost part of the tree. The robins and Cedar Waxwings enjoy these in abundance and become intoxicated if they devour too many in a short amount of time. They become a little slower and wobble around a bit, and are even known to fall off fences. The wine does not seem to affect the deer as far as I can tell. It is a pleasure to watch several species of birds consume apples at a more leisurely pace, and there are always a few remaining on the trees in the late spring. The lower branches of the apple trees are barren by late autumn thanks to the deer. In spring, more robins return from their journey south and polish off the last few dehydrated pieces that are left scattered across the ground. Nothing seems to go to waste, just as nature intended.

I was in the fruit orchard when a deer picked up a very large pink apple from the ground and it got lodged in her mouth. I witnessed the doe lifting and shaking her head from side to side. She was having trouble breaking the fruit in half. Because of this, there was a constant stream of apple juice running down from her chin to the ground. It was quite a waterfall. She wanted to enjoy the apple, not waste it. Finally, she spit out a crumpled mess on the ground and moved away to a different tree and a smaller apple.

A few years ago, I saw that one young doe had given birth to female twins. I knew they were females because the next year, the same three came, and no antlers appeared all season. They spent the summer on a cool, cleared-off dirt pile near the roadside, hidden by trees and bushes. Another favorite location for them was by my greenhouse door. There was plenty of protective coverage in these hidden locations. The walking path to the greenhouse was just over twenty feet wide, and there stood a tall Blue Spruce in the middle: a perfect hiding spot and plenty of shade from the heat in the afternoon. Walking down the staircase to the greenhouse level, I was usually greeted by the doe resting and lying on the cold loam. Her baby fawns were so well hidden somewhere that I could not even see them even though I tried to look around for them; they surely had to be close by. Sometimes she left them for long periods of time to avoid attracting predators. The young ones were taught to keep silent for their own protection.

These are some of Henry's friends who came to visit me, and they all brought me solace. They knew they were welcome at all times in the garden's safe haven. I look forward to seeing Henry each season, knowing I can be a special factor in his life. He knows I will always be there for him and his friends.

Chapter 2
a lesson in compassion
Orangy the Orangutan

The first law of ecology is that everything is related to everything else.

—Barry Commoner, 1917

The islands of Borneo, Sumatra, and Java are mountainous and thick with rainforests. Borneo is the third largest island in the world and lies across the equator in Southeast Asia. One of the highest mountains is Mount Kinabalu, rising 13,455 feet. The rainforests have swamp areas that are diverse with many different types of fruit trees, berries, flowers, insects, and roots.

Native to Indonesia and Malaysia, the orangutan is currently found only in the forests of Borneo and Sumatra. They are now critically endangered in Sumatra. They are close to extinction in most areas. At the turn of the century, there existed 315,000, and now the numbers are down 92 percent. Approximately 80 percent of the tree canopy and their habitat have been destroyed by legal and illegal logging. Generally, the trees are used for pulp and making garden furniture. One research scientist has speculated the date of 2025 for complete extinction according to the research findings.

There are two types of orangutans who originally inhabited the rain forests. In these areas, the first type are known as wild orangutans, naturally living without man's interference. The second type are the rehabilitated orangutans. They have long arm spans of six or seven feet, longer than their standing height. Their weight can range from one hundred and twenty to three hundred pounds. One adult orangutan is about as strong as eight adult humans. They are not very acrobatic like the lighter monkeys. Graceful and agile yet slow, they still cover up to a mile a day through the forests and grasslands. Like the gorillas or chimpanzees who knuckle walk, orangutans fist walk. This does not seem to be a problem for them.

Their diet consists of 350 species of plants. They find it mostly near ground level, so climbing is not that necessary for them. The life span of the orangutan is around thirty or forty years. They are generally anti-social, except some who enjoy play-fighting, hide and seek, and sunbathing. They are extremely intelligent and reason well. They can remember fruiting seasons of many different trees and fruit-bearing plants. Some say they seem to prefer women over men from research studies with trainers and scientists.

At night, they sleep in nests that can be assembled in a few minutes with branches, leaves, or palm fronds. In the morning, they will eat what material is in their nest. If a heavy downpour happens suddenly, they will hold a large palm frond over their heads. Orangutans use umbrellas and smaller leaves like napkins to wipe food off their face. How clever of them!

Some are illegally captured and domesticated. They are then trained for human pleasure, and sometimes their body parts are sold for profit. The pet trade is taking a toll on orangutans, even with the help of conservation groups and government intervention. The captive orangutans command high prices from zoos and also as experimental animals. Many are recaptured and then are retrained for successful rehabilitation and released back into the wild. The Honolulu Zoo is where I first met Orangy the orangutan. The palm trees were whispering in the warm sunlight that lined the rock path to the expansive gorilla cage. Sitting several hundred yards away from me, there was a pair of orangutans on a grassy knoll surrounded by many white-barked eucalyptus trees and several flowering plumeria trees. The aroma from the white flowers drifted in the air—the scent of gardenia spice.

They are the most plentiful type of flowering trees on the islands and are used in making leis. They range in color from snow white to brilliant rose, soft red, and deep wine shades that stand out among the stately palms. These flowering trees drop their silky petals each winter season on streets, staircases, and even in the sand, due to the tropical trade winds. I have seen tourists pick up the flower, breathe in the scent, and place it behind their ears. Giant bird-of-paradise also flourish here, with their showy colors of yellow, orange, red, and lavender.

The strikingly attractive Lantana bush catches the eye because of its bicolor flowers. Like the setting sun, on one flower are variations of yellow, orange, and red. Others are blue, violet, and purple. It's a hardy, pungent, and bitterly perfumed hedge that grows freely in the tropical landscape. Most creatures will stay away from Lantanas, so this makes for long-lasting plants. The gardens that surround the orangutans are also planted with ginger, gardenias, wild orchids, mock oranges, tuberose, pikake, Queen Emma lilies, and beach naupaka. This is part of the environment orangutans get to live in, and it is paradise to me.

Orangy was orange-juice-colored, with long twig-tangled hair running down along the sides of his powerful arms. He definitely was an impressive sight! A large enforced plate glass window, ten feet by ten feet, was provided for unobstructed viewing. There was an indentation with a cement pad to stand on in front of the glass. I was enjoying the landscaped scenery when only the male turned to face me. From the hill he was resting on, he lifted his body up to standing and came directly toward me. Closer and closer he came, each step purposeful and intentional. I thought he would stop to take a turn, but this did not happen. He came right to the window and stared into my eyes. Interestingly enough, I could see every wrinkle and curve of his face. This was very up-close and personal. I was enthralled as to what might happen next. He made a half turn and sat down to lean against the glass wall with his back toward me. If there were no glass between us, he would have been resting up against my knees.

I bent forward and placed my hands up against the glass behind his back. He slowly turned his neck to look into my eyes once again. The sun shone brightly on his dark eyes, which appeared transparent and at the same time like moonstones. I was moved by this eye contact. Such compassion was expressed in his eyes. *Did he have something to say to me?* He did! "Why do I have to be locked in here?" This is what I heard him say. This made me feel overwhelmed. *What could I do now?* He just kept staring at me with such a sad expression that it brought tears to my eyes. I could actually feel his pain.

I silently replied that I was sorry he was caged and blessed him. He very slowly turned as I watched him walk a few feet to the stone wall perimeter and sit down again. He leaned back toward the wall and put his head downward, looking at the grass. Twirling the grass with his dark, shiny, leathery fingers, working in the sod was what he wanted to do. His mate was still sitting on the knoll. I had to say good-bye to both of them and wished Orangy well in the years to come. To see him in a manmade prison for no reason, just for human entertainment, was disheartening. I felt completely helpless, but maybe he had been saved by a Good Samaritan. Who could say for sure?

Chapter 3
a lesson in abundance
Bouquet of Bees

BELOVED BEE … BUZZ

Bees collapsing in brown empty cases
Pollinators giving life to
Female and male growth
Silenced now in
Codes flowing through fragile bodies
Covered in toxic topaz coats
Gathered from
Genetically modified plants

Where and why have they gone?
Led by queen bee's signal of
Flight
Energy calling

Bees to "buzz off"
Distant planets call where
Colonies rise in new
Oasis of hope

Hives of crystal light
Gather nectar as
Workers build
Honeycombs of
Sun-drenched pollen
Bathing queens in liquid gold
We will return when
Earth is healed
You will hear our buzz … buzz … buzz
Spiraling in all life
By Joan Birkett

As I was walking in the garden near the Schubert Chokecherry tree that shades and stands guard over all the perennials in my garden, I stopped to admire this tree. The bronze and green leaves rustled in a gentle breeze on a blistering hot day. This tree has seedlings also known as suckers that spread in wild abandonment, sending up new shoots everywhere. For this reason, it is not one of my favorite trees to plant in a flower bed. Long, dark claw marks on the Schubert's bark are from a two-year-old black bear that climbed to the top branch last autumn. The marks serve as a reminder to me about the coming of its abundant dark purple clustered berries that need to be shaken off the tree lest I have many more chances to come face-to-face with one.

I noticed nearby several types of honey and wild bees drinking nectar from a tall, steel blue globe thistle in the distance. More than twenty citrine and black-colored bees were hardly moving. In hot sun, they sat in silence, gently swaying as the breezes moved past them. You would expect to hear the hum of many wings. On this particular sunny day, most of the bees' hind legs were heavily filled with rusty amber pollen. This was my opportunity to try something I had always wanted to do. I wanted to feel a bee's back. Where they soft or prickly? Since this was my first time touching a bee, I planned for a quick getaway. Gently, I reached forward, unafraid of any retaliation that might come. The back was surprisingly smooth and fluffy soft, and the bee did not mind at first. What happened next was such a delight.

I carefully massaged the back of one of the bees with a gentle stroke for about two seconds. The bee lifted its right leg toward me and past its own head and then set it back down on the blue thistle spines it was holding onto. I tried again, and the bee lifted the left leg up toward me this time. Did the bee think this was annoying? I would say most likely, yes. With the bee still motionless, I repeated the process. This time, both legs lifted swiftly toward me. I took that motion as saying, "Stay away, for that is enough."

I thought this experience was fascinating and educational. Since I was successful the first time, I tried it again with a different bumblebee. The same sequence of events unfolded for a second time. I repeated this experiment a few more times, with identical movements happening in sequence. Right, left, and then both legs! Without fail, each time, to my amazement, it was consistent. On one occasion, only one leg was lifted and then both were lifted. I have to confess that I was fairly confident that bees with their leg baskets full of pollen can barely fly. It was a newfound relationship built on trust and respect that the bees expressed to me that day—even though I considered it a bit mischievous. I blessed them and allowed them to continue their work in pollinating three-quarters of the earth's flowers, fruits, and vegetables.

Some visitors to the gardens have mentioned to me that they are afraid of bees. I told them that without bees, plant life would be devastated. Bees help pollinate a vast majority of our food sources. The pollination they are doing is a much valued service to healthy gardens everywhere around the world.

Giving respect to the bees by not being afraid or running or swatting at them is a step in the right direction. Those who show apprehension about bees can easily find a flowering plant and just observe their behavior. This is the grand design of nature in action, and we can appreciate her finest creatures that help us daily. I would say don't start rubbing bees in your gardens but respect the hard work that they contribute to the planet. Everyone could use a little magic in their life.

Bee Facts

☐ There are two hundred and fifty known species, and they are all vegetarians. One hundred years ago, they were brought to North

America for pollination of red clover plants. Clover is picked for herbal tea and can be made into a tincture. There are many beneficial healing properties in clover.

☐ Bumblebees rarely sting and only if attacked. They do not die when they sting. Honey bees have been recorded to travel as far north as Ellesmere Island, 880 kilometers from the North Pole.

☐ If they find a flower, it is the finest lodging to stay in overnight, for the bees know it will be ten degrees warmer inside than outside.

☐ It is said that bees should not be able to fly at all, for their wings are too small for their bodies. They have somehow overcome this aerodynamic problem. A fact presented many years ago that has since then been proven otherwise. Scientists have studied them in depth to learn how they fly.

In the early thirties a well-known mathematician met in a café with a few university colleagues and worked on some equations about bee flight patterns on the back of a napkin. This napkin was later taken as gospel on bee flight. It started a buzz of a story. For many decades, this bee flight story became a confirmed truth to be found in newspapers and magazines. With the advancement of high speed photography and computational physics, the old myth was finally dispelled. A question someone once asked was if bees can't fly, then what they are doing collecting nectar going from flower to flower on rose bushes outside our windows? The aerodynamics of four flapping wings is very complex; it is different from conventional aircraft aerodynamics. By bringing two wings flat against each other and then moving them apart, very strong vortices are produced, which can generate an unexpectedly large amount of lift. Spinning and swirling masses of air are why they fly so well. The study of bees has certainly helped in the research of our present-day helicopters. Scientists have built one that resembles a bee but it can only stay in flight for a few minutes.

☐ Once during a late afternoon tea, one lady who was listening to one of my garden lectures stayed behind. Standing at the arbor of the vine-covered exit door as we exchanged good-byes, she whispered to me, "You know, dear, why not try to talk nicely to your bees and butterflies? They will bring their brothers and sisters to visit your gardens!" I smiled as I looked at her, and I saw such a sweet twinkle in her eyes. I was moved by her statement. To this day, I keep this practice going. Continued happiness and abundance to the butterfly lady, the bee gods, and the beekeepers!

Chapter 4
a lesson in bravery
Tulip the Mallard Duck

Memory is the power to gather tulips in the winter.
—Anonymous

APRIL RISE

If ever I saw blessing in the air
I see it now in this still early day
Where lemon green the vaporous morning drips
Wet sunlight on the powder of my eye.

Blown bubble film of blue, the sky wraps round
Weeds of warm light that's every root and rod
Splutters with soapy green and all the world
Sweats with the bead of summer in its bud.

If ever I heard a blessing it is there
Where birds in trees that shoals and shadows are
Splash with their hidden wings and drops of sound
Break on my ears their crests of throbbing air.

Pure in the haze the emerald sun dilates
The lips of sparrows milk the mossy stars
While white as water by the lake a girl
Swims her green hands among the gathered
swans.

Now as the almond burns its smoking wick
Dropping small flames to light the candled grass
Now, as my low blood scales its second chance
If ever world were blessed, now it is.

By Laurie Lee
An English poet, novelist, and screenwriter.
1914–1997

After she had been missing for three weeks, I gave up hope of finding my domestic mallard of eight years. Her cage was a small shed, with thick straw bedding and a light to keep her cozy and safe from predators. During the summer months, a glacier-water-fed pond was near the wired caged area, for Tulip to swim freely in. The reflection of the bushes and trees on the pond shimmered like rose quartz in the early morning, and in the late evening it reflected turquoise blue shadows around the slate rocks from which flowed a waterfall. Both these times of the day were very tranquil.

The pond had a bridge crossing over the center of it, which made for a great shelter space, a hidden sanctuary. The predators that came into our grass fields were coyotes, dogs, and eagles. Surely one of these had to be the cause of her disappearance.

One day, the Bellmont family, returning visitors who stayed at the lodging located at my gardens were enjoying the valley and activities by Lake Windermere. Their young daughter Chantal was touring around the walkways and the pond. She reported something she thought was very important to her father, Jeff. "Please come look at the pond," she shouted. Jeff took a look and immediately yelled to Simon, the gardener.

Simon came running to see what they had found. Not sure of what it was, he decided to bring me to the pond, also. I was told of something that was poking out of the eight-inch blue plastic pipe near the water drainage area. The pipe was two feet deep and made a bend of ninety degrees that followed a long metal culvert to where the water flowed rapidly to the open water of the creek at the far end of the acreage. I asked everyone what they thought it was. No idea was the consensus. I quickly volunteered one of the men to put his arm down the dark hole with water rushing into it. He politely declined. "What a bunch of scaredy cats," I said. I could not even shame them into helping!

Disappointed with no volunteers, I took the bull by the horns. I bent down and lay flat out on the grass to steady myself over the rocks that were near the pipe. It could have been anything: driftwood or perhaps an eagle that had fallen in. Not looking forward to this at all, I decided to just close my eyes and shove my arm into the dark hole with water that was under extreme pressure and grab hold. I secured something, squeezed tightly, and yanked on the object. It was cold, slimy, and heavy, and I threw it into the air. It flew at least several feet upwards and landed on the grass behind us. Everyone was amazed. Was it a stray duck or my Tulip? It was hard to tell because it was thoroughly covered with green and black slime. It was happy for sure, flapping its wings and parading around, saying, "Thank God. You sure took your sweet time to find me." I said I was sorry for the predicament she had been in, but maybe next time she would be more careful. I was sure she would never go near that pipe again. The webbed feet were completely covered in muck. The normal color of a mallard duck's feet is orange, and these feet were definitely painted black.

We talked for a while and concluded, after watching her in amazement at the awful appearance of this sad duck, that it was brave Tulip. Her will to survive was clear, and she was known from that day forward as Tulip the Great. She'd spent one month in the cold blue pipe. Tulip endured chilly temperatures, swirling water, lack of food, and loneliness. I realized she had just enough air to breathe without drowning because the pond was not running at full capacity. She was siphoning off whatever food bits floated into the tube for the thirty days of confinement she'd endured. It was not her usual fare of flies, insects, wasps, grains, corn, and some grasses. Certainly water was sufficient.

We were all delighted that the missing Tulip was safe and alive. If anyone had decided to flush the pond and pull out the top piece of pipe, she would have been washed away down the metal culvert with hurling speeds of two hundred gallons per minute. She would most likely have broken something or even perished in the creek. This was one lucky ducky saved by five-year-old Chantal. Unfortunately, Chantal's mother Tamara had missed all the excitement but enjoyed our astonishing story later on.

Tulip's second adventure came one late fall a few years later. Tulip's winter cage and shed was having a few last-minute repairs, including new insulation, sheets, and a trouble light, to make sure it was secure, warm, and dry. These are the ingredients for a happy duck. I knew we were expecting a really hard frost. I thought to myself that I could surely leave her outside for one more night. The pond would not freeze solid for some time yet. Then tomorrow she would be locked in for the winter. In the early morning, I went to the top edge of the pond and noticed that the small amount of water that was open water at the bottom last night had today completely frozen solid, something I did not believe could happen, but it did. Tulip was not to be found. I searched all around. Since she was a domesticated duck, her wings were bred to be shorter so she could barely fly far enough to get out of harm's way. Flying short spurts of twenty feet was about as far as Tulip could travel. She was gone.

There was a larger creek across the gravel road a few hundred feet away from her garden pond. I decided to follow the creek down to the lake, which was difficult to do because of all the brush and blow down and the turns the creek makes. I did not see any feathers or any traces of webbed footprints. I jumped into my car and in five minutes was at the lake. Sure enough, in the bay area at the lake there were some geese, ducks, and Tulip. She stood out like a sore thumb because she was double the size of a wild mallard. Usually by this time they have all gone south. It was close to the third week in November. By mid-November, it is in the minuses, the wind is blowing, and gray has replaced the lovely autumn skies. There are just a few remaining stragglers left behind—those born late or possibly injured somehow. I tried calling her name and setting a bucket of grain out where she could see it. She was not interested. She had the largest pond ever, an expansive lake. At home, she just had a miniature swimming pool in comparison. She had found heaven.

It was getting dark, and I decided to give up and try again the next day. The lake would not freeze over completely for several weeks. That night, it froze hard again. I left at sunrise for the lake. Tulip was not moving, just standing there … or should I say stuck in the ice. She had worked her way too close to shore during the night. This situation would require drastic measures to save her. I recruited the services of Jeremy, an avid outdoorsman. Keith, one of our caring neighbors living across the street from shore, saw us and came out to help. With Keith's lent canoe in Jeremy's hand and an axe for breaking the ice, Jeremy worked his way to Tulip. An hour later, she was on her way to the shore along the open water path Jeremy had so nicely axed through the thin ice. I kept calling out to her, and Jeremy kept guiding and coaxing her with his oar raised high in the air. He had quite the long-winded conversation; I could hear Jeremy coaching her along. Jeremy was doing a superb job until she got within a few feet of the rocky shoreline.

I had to act quickly, for it looked like Tulip was turning around and going back out into the open water. I had broken away most of the ice at the shoreline while waiting for Jeremy. At just this moment, I took a running lunge out from the shore, lost my footing, and slipped into the freezing water, managing to hold on to her tail feathers as we both fell down, I on top of her, in the shallow, icy water. She let out a screeching squeal. I hung tightly onto her body. Amazingly, Carol, our local dog control officer, had arrived on the scene by some great miracle. She yelled out to me and was coming quickly with a net in hand while carrying a small dog in her arms. She threw the net securely over the duck. It landed squarely on Tulip. Great shot! Luckily, Carol patrols the area looking for stray animals and just happened to be at the beach when we needed her the most. Tulip was a very lucky ducky that we were all at the right place at the right time.

I climbed out of the water shivering, and Jeremy was now close to shore. Stepping out of the canoe, he had arrived safely. Jeremy returned the canoe to Keith, and Tulip was now wrapped in a blanket and being taken to Carol's car. The decision was made then and there to let Tulip live with Carol and her other ducks in a much larger pond that does not ever freeze. What did Tulip have to say about this decision? Not very much since her mate was killed by a coyote many years ago. She would now have many new friends to be with. She did not put up a fuss. It was for the best and I could visit her anytime.

Tulip was happy and contented and appeared none the worse for her adventure. Also noted by Fran, our nature editorialist for the newspaper, this was Tulip's second recorded adventure and the last one, as far as we knew.

Tulip had two friends who would visit at her pond only in the summer months. A mated pair of wild mallards came year after year to her peaceful sanctuary. They would spend hours in the sun together, share some grain, and enjoy each other's company. To this day, without Tulip's presence, the pair visit frequently to enjoy the pond, and I continue to feed them.

The *Alberta Calgary Herald* newspaper wrote an article on Tulip the duck. The subtitle read, "This goose isn't cooked with Chantal as her pal." Even though she was really a duck, not a goose, the words seemed appropriate.

Chapter 5
a lesson in joy
Kekaimalu the Wholphin

Kekaimalu's daughter Kawili'Kai

DOLPHIN DANCE

DOLPHINS dance and DOLPHINS shimmer,
see their spirit grow and glimmer.
Swim on, DOLPHIN, reach the top,
never look back and never stop.
The sea is calling, so dive on in,
wave that tail and raise that fin.
Give a jump for fun and glee,
then get on up and dance with me!

By Kelly Gilby

A DOLPHIN'S COMPASSION

Every day,
somewhere around the world
A dolphin reaches out to someone,
pleading for their understanding.
The day
that we listen,
the day that we reach back,
will be the day that we understand
the true meaning of trust.

By Anonymous

Swimming with the world's only known whale/dolphin was an elating experience I will not forget any time soon. The wholphin's name was Kekaimalu, and she lived at Sea Life Park on the windward side of Oahu. A tropical paradise unlike the leeward side, the windward side has nonstop trade winds and is wetter and lusher.

A wholphin or wolphin is a rare hybrid, born from mating an Atlantic bottlenose dolphin and a false killer whale. Although there is speculation that some might exist in the wild, there are currently only two in captivity, both at Sea Life Park. This first ever born was in 1985. These two species had shared the same pool for years and were not known to mate.

This changed when Kekaimalu was born in captivity and then was known to be fertile herself. She gave birth to a calf, which died within a few years. Once again in 1991, Kekaimalu had another calf but would not nurse. It was hand-reared but died at the age of nine.

On December 23, 2004, she gave birth to a third calf, a daughter, Kawili'Kai. This time, the calf nursed, and today they both remain in captivity.

A vacation was planned for Hawaii in the spring of 2006, accompanied by family and friends, Claire, Andy, and Leslie. Upon checking into the hotel I made arrangements booking in a swim with the wholphin at Sea Life Park. I had enjoyed snorkeling in the ocean on a number of occasions before but this was a great opportunity to try something new. My friend Leslie decided she would be more than delighted to join me. We could hardly contain our enthusiasm, laughing and sharing our ideas together about what we thought a ride on a half whale, half dolphin would be like. We travelled from our hotel on a bus designated especially for the park. We checked into the park and received a locker for us to store our belongings. Next we were escorted to an indoor seating area with others waiting to listen to a presentation and a video about wholphin behavior.

Leslie and I now assigned to a group of seven excited tourists we made our way to the lagoon. At the lagoon, we sat on benches for our last-minute pep talk and reviews to make sure we were all in the same boat. A few trainers were ready to teach us more about hand signals, feeding, and what we might expect from our experience swimming with a wholphin.

The largest lagoon had an island in the middle, and that would serve as our swimming practice area. The dolphins swam playfully together with Kekaimalu, enjoying the interaction with human friends who were in the lagoon ahead of us. This gave our group an opportunity to observe others and to prepare us for what was to come.

Our turn came. The water was clean and clear as we were signaled into the lagoon, and it felt like the sun had surrounded us in liquid warmth. The pool shimmered with long strings of turquoise blue pearls sparkling with the movement of each softly flowing wave. There was white foam with hundreds of bubbles left behind them each time the dolphins dove in or out of the water. With each dive, they raised their powerful bodies high into the air while we were near them. Not everyone in the pool was content with mammals diving or making circles around them. One person had become paralyzed with fear. The trainers could not help her to continue on with the rest of us. Temporarily putting our activities on hold, she made her way to the edge of the pool, to a long metal platform where the rest of us were standing. She exited the pool, and we continued on with the activity. The water came to chest height while standing in the pool.

In synchronization, we finally got to use our newly learned hand signals with the wholphin. Next, each one of us got to pose for a long wholphin kiss. Kekaimalu showed such trust and affection to our group. The trainer blew her whistle, and Kekaimalu came to us so we could see the inside of her mouth as the trainer threw raw fish into her throat. She was born with sixty-six teeth, but because of a shortage of calcium as a newborn, she had only three worn-down teeth left in her gigantic mouth. The throat was a mauve pink that she showed off proudly. How often do you get to see the inside of a wholphin's mouth, unless, of course, it is laughing at you? She showed us next that she could do this, too. Her loud, squeaking noises did sound very much like human laughter! Instead of the *ha* of humans, they make an *ek* sound.

Then we got to feel her skin with outstretched hands as she slowly glided by each one of us. It had the silkiest soft feel to it, a feeling anyone would not mind touching time and time again. Because she was half whale, she was much larger than a dolphin and her head was darker and rounded, not pointed like a dolphin's. The blow hole at the top of the head emits a tremendous burst of power and noise.

The first out in the lagoon swim was to be on a boogie board. We left the metal platform together and dog-paddled with our boards out to the center and waited. We could not see the wholphin for she was deep below us. The trainer signaled the wholphin. With our outstretched legs floating in the water, she pushed each one of us in turn, using her nose placed on the arch of our foot, across the lagoon in one continuous wavelet of spewing water until we reached the other side. This sensation felt like what I believe surfing is like. I have only body surfed without the board. With water rapidly swirling around my body, completely drenched with hair dangling, I had a big grin on my face. I have to say it was one of the fastest rides I had ever experienced. I was ecstatic beyond words. This produced the most blissful effect my nature had so far experienced. The next ride proved to be more difficult.

Saving the best for last, Kekaimalu would now swim to us upside down; then we were to reach out with our arms straight and take hold of her pectoral fins and hang on for dear life while lying on her stomach. Each one of us flew with supersonic speed, cutting through the waves swiftly like a knife through butter. The waves swirled like lazuli blue watercolors and the richest shade of pyrite shimmered with golden inclusions. It made a memorable picture for us.

The beauty, grace, and speed of this powerful mammal will stay in our minds forever. It was a thrilling experience. Truly, the wholphin is an amazing creature and has my deepest admiration showing she can interact so easily with the human species.

I made a return visit two years later to again swim with Kekaimalu. More confident and more in the moment, I felt this time I would have an extra special ride. I entered the aquamarine waters once again and chose my place next to the trainer. Many first-time wholphin swimmers were anxious but patiently awaited their instructions.

I stared into Kekaimula's little eye, so small compared to the size of her head that it seemed out of proportion. Quietly amongst all the commotion of the others around me, I took a deep breath and asked a question that I had planned in advance. I silently whispered, "What do you see in the future?" I said this with all the calmness and sensitivity I could muster.

Her reply came instantly. "It does not matter. We are all in this together." A silent message from Kekaimalu was the true message, and it made a lasting impression on me.

It has been said that dolphins and wholphins emit a pulse wave that can heal the depression of many a soul. Researchers have proven that mammals seek out humans who are feeling low. They literally go out of their way to encourage humans to be happy. It is a form of true love, sympathy, and healing that comes naturally to them.

Chapter 6
a lesson in trust
The Hawaiian Zebra Dove

ON THE WINGS OF A DOVE

I stood in the parlor
watching their arrival
as they sought a safe home
to ensure their hatchling's survival

They flew in and out
returning each time
a twig in their beaks
and cooing sublime

The patio is sheltered
No rain enters there
and the fan so high up
perfection for the pair

Their nest built and comfy
they settled in tight
and covered the eggs
all day and all night

And then it happened
The miracle occurred
The hatchlings came forth
Tiny wings on a bird

Nature is mystical
and brilliant with love
and brought us such joy
on the wings of a dove

Anonymous

Sitting outside on the sun-bleached lanai, lying in my lounge chair facing the ocean, I observed the cloud formations. The papery bright pink petals of the bougainvilleas branches were in full blossom, gently swaying, as were the abundantly fruited tangerine trees. There was a luscious citrus scent wafting through the air as the palm trees rustled in the warm breeze, and it delightfully entered my veranda. The islands have many beautiful flowers and unusual and interesting species of avifauna.

I was awakened from my reverie by several unique sounds in the shrubbery below my lanai. "Cheery-cheery-chee." It was the Red-Whiskered Bulbul. It became established on the island as a result of an unauthorized cage release around 1965. This bird has a black tuft on its head and a crimson eye patch, a creamy mocha body with a snow white belly, neck, and cheeks. The venting or the underneath parts of the tail are orange-red, so when it flies, it is a thing of beauty and is hard to miss. It travels in small flocks and feeds on fruits, berries, and insects. The female Bulbul creates a cup nest that is tightly woven but is expanable for the new growing fledglings. It dislikes salt water, so why was it here? Since flying over water is not its cup of tea, it does not populate any island other than Oahu.

The Spotted Dove that is prevalent on the islands was introduced from Asia in the mid-1800s. They eat a variety of grass seeds and inhabit native forest areas. They have a series of three to four coos, lower pitched and louder than the call of the Zebra Dove. They are almost always found eating together. The cooing continues for many hours. Early morning and just before sunset are the nosiest times.

The Zebra Dove is common on all islands from sea level to four thousand feet. It has a rosy belly, bluish-gray face, and a white-tipped tail. This tame dove feeds mostly in grassy areas but is quick to accept food from humans.

Several Spotted and Zebra doves flew onto my lanai railing. I had some raw sunflower seeds in the kitchen, so I went to find a few to share with the birds. It is recommended not to feed the birds. This can disrupt their eating patterns. For a moment, I became a rule breaker.

On previous visits to the islands, I observed many birds with tangled toes and swollen and deformed feet. Is Hawai'i so populated by humans that the hair falling out of our heads onto the ground is getting caught in their toes? This question had bothered me for some time. How could this happen? Then a light bulb went on. They spend many hours in palm trees. The palm leaves split constantly with the wind, creating hundreds of hairlike wires. I could see the strings dangling from the palms as I studied several.

Sitting on my lanai I noticed several with this deformity. I could see the deformed toes on all but a few. I opened the sliding glass door and put a few seeds on the floor just for fun. They came for the seeds immediately. My curious nature got the better of me. I took my beach towel and threw it on top of all six of them while they were eating. I carefully cradled one in another towel to check its toes. There was no squirming and complete calm. I am sure this had not ever happened to them before and surely I had not attempted this before either. I just felt moved to help a few birds out.

The toes were fine on the first dove, so I let it out the door to fly away and did the same with the second one. The third had oozing, swelling bulges. It sat patiently in the towel. I took my small kitchen knife and gently sawed away at the string until the toe broke free.

It was used to the toes being mangled together, so at first they stayed in that position. Then suddenly, it spread its toes back to normal! Quiet patience and a trusting nature were the gifts they gave to me. I heard their thanks by way of a song for my assistance in helping them.

Because of this wiring, many birds hop on one foot. Free toes for number three, and out the door it flew. The fourth and the fifth had the same problem of bound and tangled toes. I was able to untie them all. For the last one, the bind was so tight that when it was undone, the tiny toe dangled by a hair, bleeding. I took this last dove, sat down on the chair in the sunshine, and cradled it in my lap to see if the open wound would stop bleeding with the sun's healing rays. After several minutes, it seemed to be dry enough to release.

The next day, I had some repeat visitors, but not the sixth one. On the third day, the sixth dove returned, and I could see that the toe that had been ready to fall off was gone. Instead of four there were three, and it was healed. I was glad of this. Sometimes interfering with nature is not a good idea. I consoled myself for helping the suffering to be relieved of pain. A lot of happy cooing and a continuous jubilant song rang out, and I heard that song as an offering from them, their thanks for helping free their toes.

The Zebra Doves, all six of them came back the next morning to say, "Mahalo a nui" [mah hah' loh (W) AH' noo (w) ee]. Thanks very much.

My reply was, "O wau no me ka mahalo" [oh vau NOH" meh kah mah hah'loh]. I am, [yours] respectfully. "Aloha au ia ' oe" [ah loh' hah vau' ee (Y) AH' oe]. I love you.

Chapter 7
a lesson of innocence
Indigo the Black Bear

BLACK BEAR

On the burned-out island,
new trees shiver optimistic next to charred, stark trunks.
Morning stillness.
Paddles whispering through clear water.

In the dappled brush, a hole—
solid, black as night.

Except for the unbroken blue of the sky,
everything in this reviving forest is dotted, stripped,
variegated.
Aspens quake and shudder.
Branches cross-hatch the green.
Even solid bedrock has a face overgrown with lichen.

Ambling up the white rock face,
the dark shape becomes bear:
round ears on a sleek head turning to watch us watch.

He breaks free of brush and fear,
strolls the ridge top pigeon-toed and big as you please.
Against the northern morning blue sky,
he is an onyx bead in a bowl of turquoise.
He is pure shadow
interrupting the searing brightness of sun on water.

The night inside me remembers his darkness all day,
no matter how fiercely the sun burns above my head.

Barbara McAfee

It was around dusk on a lovely autumn day, and a there was an amethyst glow cast across the sky. I had just closed my back gate. I focused forward while walking and noticed a black mound in the grass fifty feet ahead of me. I knew that dark lump was not there a few moments ago. I accelerated my walk to a quick-paced run to the back door. I peeked out the corner of the door, and it had still not moved. This was good news. I was sure it had a fine collection of half-chewed apples under its paws while it was stretched out on the soft blanket of green grass. I was moved to call this cub Indigo. A stately, tall, wild Blue Spruce stands just a few feet away from the front door entrance to the house. I was on the top floor, which has cathedral windows facing a portion of the garden and the spruce tree. I could hear the snapping of a few branches from that tree. I peered out the window, but because it was so dark, I could not really see anything. I grabbed a flashlight and shinned it in the tree. The flash light caught a glimpse of two sparkling golden eyes. As I moved the flashlight around, I could see a very large body perched on the lower limb. More noise was coming from higher up in the tree. Again I moved the light to find another set of eyes about midway up the fifty-foot tree. A smaller black body was straddling a few branches but looked content. Still more noise came from a place closer to the top part of the tree: yet another set of eyes! A mother black bear and her two clubs were being taught to climb the tree in the cover of night or possibly bedding down.

I shut off the light but listened. Now plenty of cracking, snapping, and creaking branches broke the night's silence. I turned the flashlight on again to see mom on the ground underneath the tree, staring at me but waiting for her two cubs to make it down safely. The second one appeared to find its way down quickly, but it was not the case for the highest climber. It came down, lost its grip, and fell a few branches. It decided to go back up and try again. Up and down several times.

Mom looked upward now. The cub tried to move backward and then headfirst. It was pretty funny; I had to laugh. After approximately ten minutes of desperately trying, the smallest cub managed to land on the ground. All three of them were staring at me. I wished them well on their way. They silently departed to the back garden.

I was awakened from sleep a few nights later by a thunderous bang on my front deck porch. I knew such a tremendous loud sound had to be a bear landing. I peered out the window. One cub and the mother were already over the gate and walking on the deck. The second cub was next as it balanced its massive body on the gate and then bounced down on the other side. Three hundred pounds made a solid, loud thud, and so did one hundred pounds!

A sixty-foot-long railing wraps around the deck. The rail is eight inches wide. At the west end are two wooden flower baskets secured to the railing. From the rail, it is a fifteen-foot drop to the ground. I peered out the window, and all three bears were walking in line on my railing. So graceful and steady were their paws, but their fat bodies were bulging over the edges.

I could hardly imagine them balancing on this tight rope. They threw off large black shadows as they marched past the windows. It was an eerie sight to see. A full forty feet was traversed. Was this part of Cub Training 101? It was amusing to watch mom sitting down in my flower basket to rest. Close by, my bird feeders were lined up like soldiers. She picked up a suet cake and was licking it like a lollipop. The second cub sat in the other basket, and the troublesome last tree hugger, that I named, Indigo, had no basket to sit in. It stayed standing on the rail for a few seconds and then jumped down to the ground and waited for mom's next directions. This was the last time until spring that I saw this family. They were to go into hibernation for the winter months.

In the spring, the mother was satisfied that her two cubs knew the trail of the best food sources. They all separated and made their own ways.

It was not until late summer that a cub showed up in the garden. Some red elderberries and purple Schubert chokecherries had blown to the ground. Birds dropped bits and pieces. The large early yellow transparent apples were ready in August, so a banquet was served.

The cub would climb the stone steps to the front porch landing in the evenings. I had left out a sunflower birdfeeder. I forgot about removing the feeder at night. I awoke suddenly to a banging sound. The clock read 3:00 AM. I knew right away what it was: the feeder was being raided.

I picked up Salem, my seventeen-year-old stripped tabby cat, who was sleeping on the pillow next to me. Did I need her for protection? What was I thinking? I opened the double door to see a black fur ball standing on its hind legs. Salem locked in on the standing cub. Her ears were forward and posed in silence. We watched the cub through the glass window in the door; it had not noticed us. Was it pretending not to be aware of the door opening earlier? Its attention was fixed on a meal of black oil sunflower seeds. What transpired next caught me off-guard!

Really enjoying seeing the bear only a few feet away, we were four eyes staring in its direction. It seemed like slow motion. The bear turned its head and leaped full force like a lightning bolt at the door and hit it hard. I instinctively shut my eyes, with Salem still in my arms, and slammed the second door as hard as I could. My heart was pounding, and a bit of sweat fell on my brow. Surprisingly, Salem had not jumped from my arms, but I am sure she lost a life or two.

I did not realize that we must have really frightened the cub with our four eyes. I set Salem down, and she scurried underneath the bed and stayed there until daybreak. This was the first and last time Salem was to join me in any visits with wildlife.

The next day on the pathway to the greenhouse, I noticed some upturned pots strewn before the front door. I use the greenhouse for storage of business files, winter clothes, summer inflatable boats, and other storage boxes. I opened the door to shock and horror. Everything was turned upside down and torn apart. I inspected further, and one of the glass window panes was smashed, shards all over, and most of it was completely missing. Glass and blood were smeared everywhere. The odor was dull and rank. I had never seen so much blood. Purple-brown streaks of color were slathered on everything.

I wondered, could it have been one animal chasing another? Why had I not heard some noise? This question was answered by a friend who came by to visit that day. We observed the roof of the greenhouse had been walked on. Because this material is made of a very thin plastic, anything with any weight would have come crashing through. This was not quite the case.

What appeared to have happened was that Indigo, the little cub, had innocently walked across the roof and slid on the plastic to the edge of the greenhouse. Falling down the side wall, it bounced and crashed, breaking though the window with its bounding weight. Falling through glass in the dark, the bear panicked. Trying to find the same window it came in would have been a challenge, for there were twenty-five more possible choices. Clawing and scratching at all the items, it tried to find a way out. Such panic caused it to slice itself time and time again on the glass splinters. In the blackness, the cub found its way through the broken window, but not without leaving pools of blood behind. It jumped onto the roof next to the greenhouse, leaving a blood trail on the ground.

Since almost everything was destroyed in the greenhouse, all the contents went to the landfill for disposal. Very little was salvageable. The poor cub—what a nightmare it faced at such a young age! I did not see Indigo for a month. I assumed it had died. But one day, I came out of the house, and the cub was lying on the grass, chewing on an apple! Normally when I saw the cub, it was not so afraid and just carried on its business of eating. This time, at my very first eye contact, it leaped up and tore off, frightened to death of me, as if to say, "This human is extremely dangerous and causes me great pain." This was Indigo for sure: a huge, black, leathery swath of exposed skin was easy to see. I was convinced it had many more wounds. Would they heal in time?

I knew it had spent a month by the creek, probably rolling in mud to try and heal these massive glass punctures somehow, or whatever else they do. This was the very last time I saw the cub, for I devote most of my time outside gardening until late fall. It would have noticed when the apples were ripe on the trees, and it would ordinarily return for them.

Not a trace of any bear was found, even when the apples were on the ground. There were no visits during the fall. No grapes, berries, or other fruit trees were touched. As a final last effort to see if Indigo was still alive, I put out the bird feeders early, with plenty of suet cakes in plain sight. Nothing was touched at all. There were no traces to say a bear was around during the autumn or the winter.

I fear Indigo succumbed to painful deep wounds and died somewhere along the creek. Now it is in Mother Nature's hands, and after only two short years of life. Salutations to the little black bear!

Indigo the black bear!

Chapter 8
a lesson in courage
Miel the Canada Goose

TO CANADA GEESE

There is no traffic jam in the sky
when you spread your winds and fly
south along a boundless,
trackless pathway.

In undulating V-formation
unerringly you cross the nation,
wings waving to people far below.

Day after day,
like a precision drill team,
sun catching your feather's gleam,
in and out you weave and waver:
but never stray.

Your hoarse honking, its purpose clear,
although strident to our ear,
conveys to the flock aloft;
there's no delay.

Guided along by an unseen force,
you follow an instinctive course,
and make us beneficiaries
of this wondrous display

Belle Schmidt

One day, a young Canada gosling arrived at my door step. I really did not even know it was a goose at first! Obviously separated from its mother, only a few days old and all of three inches tall, I let it sleep in my nightgown pocket wrapped in a wash cloth the first night. The next day, I had errands to run. Wanting to see if I could get it to the veterinarian and not leave it at home, I decided to let it ride underneath my blouse. The tiny, soft webbed feet felt cool on my bare shoulder. It kept quiet because it was covered. It wanted to poke its tiny head out to nibble on my ear. I gushed. It was adorable. When I showed off the new little fuzzy bundle, not even the veterinarian knew for sure what it was.

After feeding it a mush mixture for several weeks, courtesy of Richard, the owner of the local feed store, it grew fast. At night I put a towel over the top of the cardboard box where it now lived in the kitchen. Several weeks previous, at my wit's end with all the loud, continuous honking noises (and I mean loud), I figured out the towel over the top of the box and another one directly on its body was the answer. As soon as the towels went on, there was complete silence.

Now one month old, the goose I had named Miel[1] had huge gray feet. The newborn size of one-half inch increased to a full four inches. It was decided she was a female, although it was hard to tell the difference between male and female at this age. It was time to take her out onto the backyard grass to see what she would do.

I found that for every step I took, she would take approximately the same number of steps and was never a few feet out of my sight. It was amazing how connected and close our bond was. Canada geese are known for patterning easily after humans. In time, she was left to wander and swim in the pond by herself. I came to check on her, and

---

1   *Miel* is French or Spanish for "honey." The color of a gosling (baby goose) at birth is yellow, speckled with gray markings.

she flew out of the water and into my arms. I was struggling to hold on to her because she had gained a fair amount of weight, but I managed to steady her. She tried to nuzzle my face with her long neck, and she gripped me tightly with the toenails of her feet so as not to fall out of my arms.

Many pleasant days were spent speaking together in goose babble, and many visitors to the gardens from different parts of the world enjoyed holding her. It was a very moving experience for everyone. You could see the delight and joy it brought to their hearts from the expressions on their faces. They were enthralled in the moment.

In another month, Miel was a beautifully full-grown goose. I felt she was getting too large for my small pond. I began looking for a larger one. I called a person I knew with a small lake and more acreage. We agreed to relocate Miel to the larger area and a larger family with several small children. She easily adopted the new family and was given the new name Dandelion by the children.

When I went to visit Dandelion a month later, all was well. I called out to her, and she still recognized my voice. Stephanie, a local veterinarian, had a large canoe, and two of her young children and I got in and began paddling. On the smooth, flowing water, the canoe moved ahead silently. The gentle waves washed up against the canoe like clear quartz crystals, bright and glimmering. There was Dandelion. The children shouted out and pointed in the direction of the goose. She swam to the front of the canoe to be next to me. We were all very excited to see this beautiful goose full grown. Dandelion spent some time with us, drifting around the canoe, and then swam away.

Many happy days ensued as she was given car rides, and she was even was known for jumping up to be held. When autumn approached, Stephanie and her family decided to take Dandelion to an even larger lake to see if she would fit in with other Canada geese. Questions like, "Will she fly south?" were on their minds. Dandelion was hesitant for several days, but eventually did take flight with some of the others. We all thought we would never know the end of this story.

One day the next spring, there was a honking sound in my backyard. I rushed out, and Dandelion had returned by herself, making several low passes around the garden and pond, honking away. "Here I am. I came back to see you!" I was amazed. My tears fell like rain. She landed twenty-five feet away from me on the green grass. I spoke silently to her, hoping she might understand or feel my innermost thoughts. She stayed for fifteen minutes. I positioned myself on the grass near her. After nibbling in the grass, she then took flight as I waved good-bye. What a sight to see the takeoff so close to me. I watched her graceful flight as she disappeared from view.

Later that day, I called Stephanie to let her know that Dandelion might be coming for a visit. She happened to be home. She heard plenty of honking noises also and said it must have been Dandelion, even though she did not see her. They say Canada geese never forget where they were raised and always return. She proved that. We all were grateful for this incredible experience. Would she return again? Not in the autumn that year, but next spring, my neighbor, Gail called me to say, "Your goose is in the field, honking. She wants to talk to you. Better hurry and get out there." There she was again, and I talked and blessed her on her journeys and for coming to visit me again.

The third year, I must have missed her because I cannot stay in the garden round the clock. However, I got to see her again the fourth spring in the same field, this time with a friend. I know they are supposed to have only one mate for life. Was this the one? I finally took a picture of Dandelion and her friend to add to my many wildlife collection photos from the past twenty-five years.

My Miel! Does she have still a shred of memory left for me? Research says geese never forget. I know she continues to fly skyward, with her guardian angels high above. The golden rays of the daytime sun sparkle on her back. Her wings are strong. The feathers form long strands of sparkling diamonds threaded together, which give them such strength. The evening flights bring cool, translucent, violet hues of the setting sun. Into the silver light of the moon she flies. Does she remember me?

Chapter 9
A lesson in love
The Hawaiian NeNe

My first visit to Oahu, the island of aloha[2], was when I was sixteen years old. My school friend, Susan, asked me if I would like to spend summer vacation there with her uncle. My answer: "Absolutely, yes! No doubt whatsoever." No thinking was required on this question. We were excited and spent some after school and weekend hours working at a Laundromat and cleaners to save enough for airfare and spending money. That wonderful day came to realization. We were packed and ready. Off we went on the first of July to the island of Hawaii.

Slowly, day by day, I fell more in love with the islands. I often wondered why I was not born there. I desired to return to paradise.

My most recent visit was made special by buying a Hawaiian bird identification book. I found out that many introduced birds were thriving and a few native ones were extinct.

A picture of the Canada goose aroused me because I'm Canadian. My interest overall, however, is that I have always been awed by some of the brilliantly colored birds and flowers that thrive on the islands. I listened and scanned the skies on my walks and even while swimming in the ocean. Seeing the Red-footed Booby, which feed at sea mostly at night, was a rare sight. Their brilliant fire red webbed feet stand out when flying and upon landing. Many Great Frigate birds accompany the Booby to make them disgorge their catch of fish and squid. The Frigate then catches it before it hits the water.

One of Hawaii's most common seabirds, the wedge-tailed <u>Shearwater, is s</u>een almost everywhere. They begin life in the ground

2   Aloha [Alo = presence, front, face] + [ha = breath] "The presence of divine breath." [oha = joyous affection]. It is one of the most important words in the Hawaiian language. Be careful to use the word *only* if you truly feel aloha within. Do not use it carelessly or without sincerity. On a spiritual level, *aloha* is an invocation of the divine: acknowledgment of the divinity that dwells within and without. It can be thought of as single-word blessings or prayers. *Aloha* is being a part of all and all being a part of me, a true expression of love.

in holes and then spend most of their lives in exuberant flight over the open sea. They course low over the waves on stiffly held wings. They have eerie braying cries that might seem ghostly to the uninformed.

One day as I began my early morning walk, I turned my head upward. I saw at that moment four Canada geese, *Branta canadensis*, cutting through the air so smoothly like softened butter. Not a sound was heard. I stopped in my tracks and observed them until they were gone.

I began asking some of the employees at the hotel if they had ever heard or seen these geese. A very tanned local man said, "Yes, they do come on occasion, but it is usually the smaller variety that enjoy their winter vacations here on the islands." The *Branta bernicula* has a shorter neck than the Canadian version and is about thirty inches long. Sometimes people confuse these Canada geese with the common Nene goose, pronounced "nay nay," Hawai'i's official state bird that lives in barren lava regions where many berries, such as huckleberries, flourish. They have diagonal rows of white feathers and buff cheeks with deep furrows of black skin showing through, giving them a striped appearance. It is a form of air-conditioning in the hot, sunny lava plains!

He also informed me the geese sometimes hitch rides with the cruise liners. Of course they get fed until they are closer to land. Some hitchhike for only a few hours. It would be an experience on a holiday cruise to be entertained by a few winged passengers. On occasion, the real Canada geese do make a showing on the islands. I cannot blame them for their choice of holiday destination.

The first time I saw the Nene was at the majestic Makapuu lighthouse. It is located in a park high on the cliffs, overlooking the ocean. Several birds were drinking from a hose that one of the gardeners ran each day for them. Many tourists were snapping photos of these beautiful birds.

It appeared that one of the park's gardeners was watering some brightly colored Croton shrubs and then turned to fill up water buckets for the four Nene that were close to him. From my previous experience with my goose, I thought I would try saying a few "Beep beeps" or "Wheet wheets" to see if there may be any reactions. I waited until the gardener and some tourist had left that location before I began my conversations. Softly and gently bobbing my head, I repeated these sounds for a minute, and then, so sweetly, I received a reply. They expressed to me their joy at having someone care about them enough to consider them equals. I guess they figured I could be trusted, and we shared this friendly moment together. I thanked the Nene gods for this time in a silent human prayer. These geese do not have the hardship of the Canada geese, so their life in the warmer climate is their blessing.

Nene, *Branta* (neocene) *sandvicensis* has evolved from the Canada goose, which migrated to the islands five hundred thousand years ago, shortly after the islands were formed. In 1778, when Captain James Cook arrived on the island shores, more than twenty-five thousand Nenes were found. By 1950, there were only thirty geese left. They are on the endangered species list, almost extinct because of hunting by native Hawaiians, predators, and cats from European settlers. Also mongoose, pigs, and dogs feed on the eggs and the young. Today there are about five hundred wild Nenes due to successful captive breeding programs.

Abundantly living in shrub lands, coastal dunes, and higher elevations of rocky lava flows, they do not need to swim for they can gather water from fog and dew, or juice from leaves and berries. Nene is an herbivore. Male and female look identical except for size. They fly only rarely because they have weak wings. They mate for life but will find another mate if the first one is lost or dies. Their feet have evolved to have less webbing and more padding in the toes so they can traverse rough terrain quickly. They are somewhat cautious toward people but with a little coaxing they are happy to eat grain when it is offered to them.

Another Hawaiian local I met related to me a story that was published in the local newspaper of three predator birds and one prey bird getting on board a cruise ship docked in a harbor. They all stayed on board the entire way to the next harbor. The predators never captured their prey during the whole voyage, even though there were close encounters. The passengers were kept highly entertained. The crew also enjoyed the visitors, with all of their antics, until they arrived at the designated harbor at sunset and witnessed a spectacular green flash on the horizon. At that same instant, the birds safely flew away. That was one lucky prey bird and one amazing sunset! Mahalo![3]

I have enjoyed over a hundred sunsets on the islands, and I finally caught a glimpse of the cyan blue and green streak the islanders call the coveted green flash. Surfers, sailors, and others who spend a lot of time on the water see this often. The phenomenon responsible for the green flash also paints rainbows.

The red image of the sun gets bent the least, so the red scatters first and then sets on the horizon. The next color, yellow, is absorbed, and then the blue and violet colors scatter and are absorbed. This leaves only the green image, which is the last color that scatters at the horizon when the sun sets completely. With no sun left to see, there is the green color, which scatters, and being last, it bends the most at sunset. At this

---

3   Mahalo [Ma = In] + [ha = breath + [alo = presence, front, face] "May you be in divine breath." It is as important as *aloha*. It is a divine blessing. The word is ineffable, indescribable, and indefinable. Say these two words often, as they can be life-transforming and -enhancing.

precise second, a green burst of light will shoot out and upwards into the sky, off the ocean. This is the green flash that everyone would like to see. If you blink your eyes, you could miss it. So look for the coveted green flash at sunset on your next island vacation.

Aloha 'oe!

May you be loved!

Chapter 10
A lesson in curiosity
Rufous the Hummingbird

The hummingbird is the smallest and most delicate-looking bird on the planet. It could be considered a glorified bee. The smallest near-threatened hummingbird species is the bee hummingbird. This bird is not a bird at all but a pink and gray moth that usually appears only at sunset. The smallest of the hummingbird species is only two inches, and the largest species can measure up to eight inches in length. Their wings beat at a rapid rate of up to two hundred times per second. The second fastest of all animals on earth, this exquisite-colored bird's head is red and pink, and it has a blue body. The under parts are a grayish white. Their populations are dwindling due to a loss of habitat.

The energy from their wings creates extreme vibrations. Their body can be seen clearly and the wings are a blurred flutter. When flying, they have been clocked at speeds of thirty-five miles per hour. This allows them to reach a constant speed of thirty miles an hour, which can be maintained for more than two hundred feet without much effort. They are considered by scientists to be the smallest rocket ships on the planet. They can lock in flight speeds even up to sixty miles per hour for short bursts if necessary to escape from danger.

During courtship the male hummingbird makes a straight line upwards, using great momentum and speed to reach elevations of over one hundred feet. Then he takes a split second pause hovering in the air before his dive downward, following that same straight line. After nearly breaking the sound barrier, he will come to a complete standstill, flutter his wings to impress a female, who is close by and is watching his aerobatics. This performance is repeated two or three times. The males, who can deliver this maneuver three times will show they are compatible and worthwhile mates. This is called the hummer's dance. They can also fly upside down, sideways, backward, and in a figure eight pattern. These tiny birds are built for flight, with their light hollow bones and huge breast muscles that capture an abundance of air.

One day, I collected some herbs with tubular bell-shaped flowers that are a lovely shade of coral, copper, and orange. The botanical name for this herb is *Agastache firebird* or Hummingbird Hyssop, and it is edible. I was turning around after picking an abundant bouquet for my vase, and at the same time I raised my hand to my nose to take pleasure in its vanilla and anise aroma. This bunch of copper bells caught the attention of a feisty Rufous hummingbird.

There he was, humming in midair while he was enjoying the nectar of the tubes right in front of my eyes. A male with a red-gold iridescent throat and chin! I studied every vibrational movement of the wings and feathers while remaining motionless. After drinking from at least a dozen flowers, it soared off and out of sight in a blink of an eye. I held my gaze steady to see it land on a tall Blue Spruce close by. It was a moment to treasure. I continued turning to take my bouquet into the house when he returned again for a second treat. For me, it was another chance to whisper something meaningful to this hummingbird. The best surprise of all came a few seconds later. The mate came zooming out of the spruce and was now enjoying the flowers I held also, a female with a greenish-gold crown and back. I had two for the price of one. I was happy to accommodate their wishes, holding the nectar for them. Time seemed to stand still when the three of us were together. It was a great feeling to help these tiny supersonic jet airplanes to a nectar lunch.

I was watering some daylilies in the rose garden later on in the day when a hummingbird appeared before me. It stopped at the point where the water comes out of the nozzle. The spray of water had an arch of about ten feet. This time, a black-chinned hummingbird dropped down onto the spray and took a water slide ride. I had read that these gorgeous birds can be really playful, curious, and ingenious. It returned many more times to play with me and get a refreshing shower. They have been known to hang upside down on a branch to shake the water off more quickly.

During the week of Wings over the Rockies[4], I have in the past given a presentation on the history and migration of hummingbirds. This event was shared by Elizabeth, another enthusiastic horticulturist friend of mine. In an outdoor garden setting, visitors came to sit in the sun with their binoculars and telescopes while listening to a discussion on the life of hummingbirds. I have a variety of different types of feeders

4   Wings over the Rockies is a week-long event with many activities for people to enjoy bird watching.

hanging in the trees. These feeders will help to hopefully attract some hummingbirds for others to see up close and personal. I am happy to report that at each past event, we were lucky enough to have had several successful sightings.

While speaking, Elizabeth noticed a hummingbird dart past her and fly into the open door of the tea house. She brought this to my attention. She continued speaking, and I went inside to try and retrieve the trapped hummingbird. I should have learned by now that keeping bunches of colorful silk flower arrangements inside the room can be irresistible to them, especially the juveniles. Juveniles will fly up to stop signs, red baseball caps, and most anything red. They are not as experienced as their parents. I usually have a butterfly net handy for just such occasions. I was not able find it this time for occasionaly it is kept in the garden shed outside. Hummingbirds can expend themselves of energy quickly when frightened, so time is of the essence in securing them for release.

I quickly cupped my hands and zoomed in on the madly panting bird. I held it gently against the window pane. When I felt it was secured, I carried it gently outside. I wanted to show the visitors this tiny creature as they moved in close for viewing. I slowly opened my hands. The head was the size of a marble, and it stood perfectly still for all to witness.

In just a few more seconds, I opened my hands fully, giving it complete space. It definitely was not in a rush to fly away, though. It needed to assess the situation it was in and regroup itself. Maybe it was taking its time to thank each and every admirer? With lightning speed, it blasted off the landing platform of my hand to freedom. In doing so, it left a tiny feather falling gracefully to the ground. Several guests watched it fall and searched for it in the tall grass without any success. It was lost forever and returned to Mother Earth, the true owner of these things.

First thing in the spring, I set out newly flowering bright red geraniums, Japanese flowering maples, Lantanas, and yellow and pink daisies. To add to these flowers were red and orange silk gladiolas tied to a post or in a plant pot in plain sight for viewing. This was a beacon to attract them from up to a mile away! These flowers and silks tend to direct the males to the colors they love the most. The males arrive two weeks before the females. It is their job to find the best possible nectar locations that will be plentiful all summer long.

I always use a white cane sugar mixture as the old-fashioned red-food-colored ones have been known to cause liver failure and make them sick. New varieties of naturally colored sugars are available now. Several hummingbirds can share one location, but it is recommended to have few different feeding stations. This is because they are quite territorial.

They take insects out of spider webs or catch them in midair if need be. Since their hearts and wings beat several hundred more times than any other creature on this planet, they use up a lot of energy getting their food and nectar. At dusk, they have the last meal for the day. Finding a hiding spot to sleep at night is easy for them. Near the trunk of a tree will do nicely and holds more heat and less wind than near the end of a branch.

Before they were named hummingbirds, they were called resurrection birds. The reason for this was because they can completely slow their heart beats to a very low rate. It is a hibernation-type deep sleep that is called torpor. While in this deep sleep, their beaks face upward. Because they were observed sleeping this way, many thought they died at night but then miraculously came to life in the morning. Once awake, they are slow to start their engines, like some humans I know. This is how they came to be known as resurrection birds.

Hummingbirds migrate along corridors of several mountain ranges. Some leave for Mexico in the winter and fly all the way to Alaska in the summer. Twenty varieties appear all over the world. For many, it is a three-thousand-mile trip. They will fill up on nectar for a few weeks until their weight is that of a dime. Then they fly approximately five hundred miles and lose most of this weight when they have completed their journey. They repeat this process until they reach their final destination. The average life span is three to seven years. One of the oldest known banded hummingbirds was said to be thirteen years old.

The eggs are the size of peas. The nests are usually difficult to see and made of lichen, moss, bark, feathers, cotton, and many other man-made and natural materials, including spider webs. The silk is an important part because when the young ones grow, the nest expands with them because of the elasticity. The longest known web string reported in a hummingbird's nest was measured at one hundred fifty feet long.

Since spiders multiply so abundantly, there are plenty of web strings to be found without jeopardizing them. Spiders can remake webs in a very short time and can spin their own parachutes to lift themselves up into the air stream. It is easy for them to float along, landing anywhere they please just by letting some air out of their chutes. If you could look up with microscopic eyes, there would be thousands flying over your head. It is probably best that we do not have these kinds of eyes. This is how they come to land on our clothes, and we bring them inside our homes. I do not squash the life out of them. Using a cup and a plate for the lid and releasing them outdoors where they can continue to serve and work for the planet is best for them.

Predators do watch other predators, so if you see a bird's nest, walk right past it. Look at the nest from a distance, because another predator could be watching you. Sneaky predators abound.

There is a famous story about the Alaska hummingbirds receiving a free flight to Mexico, paid for by caring citizens. These birds spend only two months of summer in Alaska. This is all that is available to them before the environment around them starts to freeze and they must make the long flight south. Why they bother going to Alaska is a real mystery. Perhaps there are a lot of wild flowers along a secret route.

One year, citizens became concerned that if the birds did not leave at the usual time, they might all die. A group of avid birders decided to take immediate action. Nearly one hundred hummingbirds were caught and secured in protective boxes. An airline company agreed that if a ticket was purchased for them, they would get delivered to their homes in Mexico. So the story went, and there was a very happy ending indeed.

Chapter 11
a lesson in loyalty
Salem the Cat

With silent footsteps in the night,
Knowing I sleep the tormented sleep
Of someone searching for the light

With gentle touch upon my face
Tracing the tracks of my now dried tears
And filling what once was empty space

With shallow breath so near and dear
She pauses, patient in her quest
Sensing her warmth is needed here

Watching me with troubled eyes
Knowing there is no cure for what ails me
Excepting time, but still she tries.

My cat comforts me.

By Carole K. Boyd

This chapter is dedicated to ailurophiles everywhere who love and understand the mind and spirit of the cat.

A great discovery was recently found in an excavated anthropological site in Cyprus. A nine-thousand-five-hundred-year-old skeleton of a cat and a human had been buried together. Even dating back this far, cats were considered exalted souls or guides for humans.

In Norse mythology, the goddess Freyja, symbol of love and fertility, is depicted riding a chariot drawn by cats. It was believed cats were a symbol of good fortune and can be seen in drawings and sculptures throughout the ages.

Dearest Salem (or Sailey, as she is so fondly called) is a miniature, seven-pound, seventeen-year-old tabby. She looks like a downscaled tiger. Most of her fur markings are marbled or, as I amusedly call them, perfectly polka-dotted. To add to her charming features, she has a white tuxedo chest and out-of-this-world apple green eyes. Green is also the color of the heart chakra associated with love. Living with a loving, balanced heart can bring overall good health, growth, and prosperity.

She also has another nickname of Squeaky, for when held or squeezed, she lets out a one-note squeak sound. She is frisky and an agile gymnast, like so many cats are. She has a fondness for small silk flower tops and enjoys playing catch like a dog. One day, I noticed her carrying one flower top around in her mouth. I wondered, *What if I took one of these flowers and tossed it at her? Could she catch it?* She sure did! To increase the challenge, I threw the flower up through the oak railing. It landed on the carpet on the top floor. She raced up, secured the flower, came back down the staircase, and literally spat it out at my feet. *Remarkable*, I thought. *I will try this game again to see if it will work, to see if it wasn't just a one-time coincidence.*

We kept the game going. It played on over a dozen times. She enjoyed playing. I kept her practicing by throwing the tops two times each session. I was anxiously waiting for my family to visit to share Salem's new talent. She did not disappoint me, and the games were great fun for all to see. Soon the flowers were disappearing. I found several underneath sofas and hidden behind curtains when vacuuming. As time passed, all the flowers went missing, and I figured she was telling me she was absolutely done with this game and I had better think up another one.

Salem is an indoor cat, and we share quality time each day. I ask her to let me know how she is feeling and what she would like to do. I try to improve my communication skills with her all the time. Salem's talking is what I call love chatter, sounds that are not in the normal cat vocabulary—for instance, the sound *fur now* with a higher pitched tone with the now part. She can repeat this sound several times in a row, and I tenderly try to emulate it. I let her decide when she is done with her conversations with me. For now and always, we will have a loving companionship and deep connection. Cats are amusing and will put a smile on your face. The busiest of worlds can be left behind by spending some quiet, precious moments in their company. They say cats need ten minutes a day of human contact to remain in a healthy state.

I was working on a research paper for my world religions course in university. My assignment was to interview a Tibetan monk. A monastery was located in the San Bernardino Mountains outside of Los Angeles, California not far from where I lived. When I reached the monastery and went inside, it was deeply quiet, and fragrant incense was burning by a nearby altar. The interview was detailed, and I took lots of notes. Then I was allowed to see the cubicles where the monks sit facing a blank wall in contemplation for hours. When the hour was over, he gave his blessings to me with folded hands, and I bowed my head. This is the proper gesture to show that my soul bows to your soul. I asked him one last question: if he had one thing to tell me that would benefit my life and the lives of others, what would that be?

His reply was to me to be more catlike! "Excuse me?" I said. I thought for a second. Then I realized his reply made such sense. Continuing, he said, "Cats are always loving, compassionate, and meditative. They enjoy being playful and are extremely loyal. If you hurt them, they forgive you immediately. They might be afraid of you for a while, but they will always give their unconditional love." Wise and inspirational words! I came away from our meeting with a powerful sense of gratitude and inspiration that fueled my heart.

A lovely experience happened one Saturday several years later. A sunrise wedding ceremony was to take place at the gardens. Standing next to several lighted torches placed in the grass and a flower-garlanded altar, the happy couple were saying their vows. A movement overhead caught my attention. There were at least fifteen birds circling twenty feet in the air. They were there for just a few seconds and then they flew away. I was too mystified with my camera in hand to snap a shot. I watched intently instead, enjoying this entrancing scene. I thought to myself, *I wonder if anyone else is watching this?*

Standing near an overgrown flower bed and close to the flower petal path, I felt a soft brush of silky fur against my bare legs. I heard a gentle mew sound coming from Salem, who was looking upward toward sky. I believe Salem was there to tell me that she had witnessed the birds, also.

How observant and loving these furry charmers are! I give you this short "tail" in heartfelt joy and appreciation for our feline and feathered friends.

Hiss-tory: Thousands of years ago, cats were worshiped as gods. Cats have never forgotten this!
—Anonymous

As anyone who has ever been around a cat for any length of time well knows, cats have enormous patience with the limitations of the human mind.
—Cleveland Amory

I believe cats to be spirits come to earth. A cat, I am sure, could walk on a cloud without coming through.
—Jules Verne

White Plumeria
Symbol of beauty and Love

In conclusion, I have learned many things from these encounters over the years, establishing a bond with animals. They have taught me many lessons. It has been a training course in having reverence for all living things, enjoying the moments we have with them and taking pleasure in the little things, for this matters the most in life. These experiences and memories will stay with me forever. I will never know when an opportunity may come my way again to share in another adventure of this nature, but I hope it will be soon.

I am deeply grateful for all that Mother Nature has to offer. I praise her wonders, and because of her creations, I am able to share these stories with you.

LIST OF POETS

"Deer Tracks" by Henry Burt Stevens: *www.Authorsdenpage.S/Henry*

"The First Law of Ecology" quote by Barry Commoner

"April Rise" by Laurie Lee

"Beloved Bee Buzz" by Joan Birkett Invermere

"Dolphin Dance" by Kelly Gilby: *www.thedolphinplace.com/poetry*

"A Dolphin's Compassion" by Anonymous

"Black Bear" by Barbara McAfee: *www.barbaramcafee.com* copyright 2000 - 2009

"To Canada Geese" by Belle Schmidt: *www.poems.lovecanadageese.com*

"My Cat Comforts Me" by Carole K. Boyd: shgallery@hctc.net

"Cat Quotes and Inspirational Thoughts" by Cleveland Amory

"Jules Verne and Gandhi"

Additional Resources

Cayce, Edgar. *The Power of Color, Stones and Crystals*. New York, NY: Grand Central Publishing, 1989.

Fayt, Elisabeth. *Paving It Forward*. Calgary, Alberta Canada: Morgan James Publishing, 2009.

Goldberg, Natalie. *Writing Down the Bones*. Boston, Massachusetts: Shambhala Publications, Inc., 2005.

Hanson, Harold C. *The Giant Canada Goose*. Champaign, Ilinois: Southern Illinois University Press, 1997.

Harris, Bill. *Thresholds of the Mind*. Beaverton, Oregon: Centerpointe Press, 2007.

Kidd, Sue Monk. *The Secret Life of Bees*. New York, NY: Viking, 2002.

Manuel, Elizabeth, B.Ed. *Cace Living with the Angels*. Edmonton, Alberta: 1ˢᵗ Impressions Publishing, 2006.

Melchizedek, Drunvalo. *Living in the Heart*. Flagstaff, Arizona: Light Technology Publishing, 2003.

Roads, Michael J. *Talking with Nature*. Tiburon, California: H J Kramer Inc., 1987.

Schultze, Kymythy R. *Natural Nutrition for Dogs and Cats.* Carlsbad, California: Hay House Inc., 1999.

Sladen, F.W.L. *The Humble Bee.* Herefordshire, England: Logaston Press, 1912.

Taylor, Terry Lynn. *Messengers of Love, Light and Grace.* Tiburon, California: H J Kramer Inc., 2005.

Virtue, Doreen PhD. *Healing with the Fairies.* Carlsbad, California: Hay House Inc., 2001.

Yogananda, Paramahansa. *Autobiography of a Yogi.* Los Angeles, California: Self-Realization Fellowship, 1943.

SAVE THE ANIMALS ORGANIZATIONS

Defenders of Wildlife, WA, DC, USA: www.Defender.org

IFAW.CA, Canada, International Fund for Animal Welfare: www.Ifaw.org

WWF World Wildlife Fund: www.Worldwildlife.org/Species

Greenpeace in Canada Support.Greenpeace.Ca: www.StopSealHunt.ca

Greenpeace in United States: www.Greenpeace.Org

Turn the Tides: Oceana.org/North-America/Home/

Author's Biography

I was given my first real gardening job at the age of eleven years in the sixth grade at Westwood Elementary School in Los Angeles, California, my place of birth. My teacher seemed to notice that I was touching and dusting off with my fingers some of the live plants that were located in the hallways. There must have been talking behind my back because one day the vice principal approached me and asked if I wanted to water and clean the school's hanging pathos vines and waxy-leafed philodendrons. I would be allowed out of class if I finished my assignments early on Fridays. An opportunity to get out of class was an excellent offer. So started my love of green things.

After school, I rode the bus to my home. I had to walk down a short alleyway where I entered a metal gate attached to a white picket fence that surrounded our property. Through the gate, up a steep staircase was a slight hill where my grandmother lived in a home on our property. One had to go past and around her victory garden. Victory gardens were introduced after World War II by Eleanor Roosevelt to help people grow their own food. Michelle Obama has started an organic garden, including beehives for honey and pollution. She feels her garden will be an example for people to reconnect themselves with growing and working in harmony with nature.

There were all types of vegetables and many tea roses in grandma's victory garden. I used to admire them and was amazed by the colors and fragrances of the large hybrid roses in bloom. In a two-acre vacant lot next to my home was my father's garden. His specialty was to grow all types of delicious melons. He did it for fun and was dedicated to attending them. They were a very special treat at the end of the hot summer. I feel I had a great opportunity, growing up surrounded by and appreciating nature.

Early in the mornings in July and August, our grandmother, Mena, would take my brother, George, and I on the Pico Boulevard bus for a twenty-minute ride to Santa Monica Beach. The beach, with its famous pier, had a Ferris wheel, the kind with ornately decorated horses and gold-ringed poles that moved to organ music. There were beach-wear shops, artists, ice cream stands, and a fish market. We would walk along the hot asphalt-paved stretch of pier with our hair blowing about with the salt-sprayed air. Seagulls flying and catching thermals danced around us with their usual chatter. We were excited to stop for our lunch at the fish market. Here lay mounds of shaved ice that filled the cooler; fresh crab and shrimp cocktails were beautifully displayed. The man behind the counter handed us the snow cone paper cups filled to the brim with pink shrimp on shaved ice with plenty of homemade sauce. All our fish was wrapped in brown paper, folded in the way that florists wrap long-stemmed roses.

We walked down the splintering wooden staircase to the sand to find our place for the rest of the day. Once our beach towels were laid out, we ate our lunch in the warm sun. We were close to the water's edge, where the liquescent foam would just touch our toes. We would carry buckets of sand, water, and sifters to our designated location to make projects for the day. When the waves washed out off the shore, we would watch the holes in the warm sand for bubbles so we knew where the sand crabs were hiding. After scooping up the crabs, we watched them swim around in colorful metal pails as the sand settled to the bottom. The sound of the waves crashing in the distance and splashing against the barnacled poles that supported the pier filled the air with melody. After an hour making sand castles, we could hardly wait to splash around and swim in the ocean. Such simple pleasures filled our carefree days for many summers.

Being somewhat shy in junior high school, my parents thought it would be a wonderful idea to enroll me in acting classes after school. In walking distance from my home was the 20th Century Fox movie studio. Located in close proximity to the studio was a small theater house for budding actors of all ages. After school and on weekends, I would take part in skits, learning facial expressions and reading lines for an upcoming play entitled *The Martians Have Landed*. I got my first part playing a Martian queen's daughter. It was truly an enriching experience I will never forget.

Most remember the dance television show *American Bandstand*, hosted by Dick Clark. An opportunity came along one Saturday afternoon to take part in the show with my brother George. He and his friend David Cassidy, actor and singer of the famed *Partridge Family* show on television used to get together as we lived not far from each other in the same neighborhood.

Living in West Los Angeles was a great opportunity to run into a few glamorous Hollywood stars. In my early years, while I was working in Beverly Hills as a cashier in a movie theater, in walked Elvis Presley. He was ten minutes late with two friends in tow. They were also the first to leave at the end of the movie so no one would know they had ever been there.

On an afternoon shopping spree with a girlfriend, we approached the first floor parking lot elevator of the Century City Mall in Beverly Hills. We went up to the second floor, and when the doors parted, in walked Cher of Sonny and Cher fame. Hellos were exchanged. We did our best not to go crazy and say something stupid, so we stood in silence. All four of us got out on the third floor.

My most memorable moment escorting Hollywood celebrities Elizabeth Taylor and Richard Burton, along with John Houston, to their theater seats. They were attending the premier of *Cleopatra*. I was an usher at the Westwood Theater on the weekends. I was able to speak with Mr. Houston for a moment. He directed and acted in many great historical movies.

As we entered the era of the hippies, peace, love, ecology, and brotherhood, I worked at a famous plant store named Mother Earth. My first job was making terrariums with miniature plants inside glass containers. Landscaping inside bottles was extremely popular for many years, bringing with it a bit of nature indoors.

Many holidays were spent on the Hawaiian Islands. Enjoying time in this tropical setting gave me an even greater appreciation of how beauty and nature blend together so eloquently in many different ways. Around every corner would be an exotic flowering visual delight, with birds happily darting about. Hidden underneath sweet, aromatic, tropical foliage, you could hear the sound of cooing doves. These scenes, along with brown-skinned surfers, colorful surf boards, and dolphins playing together in the iridescent blue waves on the ocean are the memories permanently imprinted in my mind.

I studied horticulture during this time at a few colleges and ended up with a degree. Thereafter, I transplanted myself, in the care of a new partner, to British Columbia, Canada.

Canadian gardening is challenging and rewarding at the same time. After many years of building up a landscaping business, I opened up our acreage to the public for garden tours and weddings.

What I have learned in my life that made these subsequent stories so meaningful was to be sincerely open to the joyful discovery of nature's beautiful creations. A gift of the intricate sounds, colors, and patterns of the bounty of nature awaits anyone, right at their doorstep.

I am a graduate of Santa Monica College, holding a Horticulture degree from UCLA in California. I facilitate workshops, do research work, and have been an instructor for botanical gardens, all of which has put me close to nature. I have worked for the Forestry Service in British Columbia, Canada, on research projects for Pine Beetle and wildlife identification. My latest non-fiction work in progress is about the *transformation of V*, a brave Canada goose who I raised from a few days old, and how it learned to fly south.

Christiana and the author at Hawaiiana Hotel in Waikiki